DOG FOOD RECIPES

THE

DOGS

DINNER

How to Prepare Nutritious and Healthy Meals for Your Dog

Jane Romsey

Published by Fat Dog Publishing LLC in 2016

ISBN: 978-1-943828-44-9

This book is dedicated to my beloved dogs
Lulu and Pebbles.

Thank you for bringing so much joy
into my life and for making me laugh every day!

Contents

How to Use This Book

This book was created with one main goal in mind: to educate the loving dog owner about how to create healthy meals for his or her pet dogs. Obesity and other health problems arise in dogs because of poor meals and diets, which is why this book has a cautionary tone when it comes to giving your dogs table scraps and human food items. The first part of this book covers a comprehensive range of topics so that you have complete knowledge of your dog's nutritional needs.

The three major macronutrients are covered in the sections "The Truth About Proteins," "Should Fats Be Avoided?" and "Carbohydrates in a Dog's Diet." Mineral supplementation is also covered in detail in the first part of the book, right after the section "In Focus: Micronutrients." You can find out more about foods that are harmful to dogs by reading the section "Danger Ahead: Foods That Are Toxic to Dogs." For owners of senior dogs with feeding problems, you may want to skip ahead to the section "Feeding Older Dogs: The Puzzled Owner's Guide."

All the recipes for homemade meals can be found in Part 2 of the book. Part 2 of the book has three sections: "Treats Galore", "Using a Dehydrator" and "Snacks and Quick Meals."

NOTE:
Most of the recipes are rice free and they are marked with a *
in the contents section.

Part 1: Introduction

Coming from a family of animal lovers – my parents, brothers, sisters, and I cared for a variety of animals since I was young, including a lot of dogs – I was naturally fascinated with the idea of providing optimal care to domestic pets, most especially dogs.

For a very long time, people have been walking into pet stores and coming out with puppies without any idea about how to provide the optimum care for their new pets.

One of the central principles of optimum dog care is good nutrition. You might be surprised when you find out about the actual needs of our canine companions. The answers to questions about dog nutrition cannot be found on labels of dog foods – in fact, that's the last place you should be looking if you're uncertain about your dog's daily nutritional needs.

If you want your dog to live a long, active, and happy life free from the common health problems associated with modern dogs (who are fed the wrong food every day), then this book is definitely for you.

Contained within these pages are insights and discoveries that I have made through the years, as I've taken care of multiple canines. It is a gift to the present and future generation of dog lovers who know how precious the companionship and love of dogs really are. This is for you, my dear friend. Welcome to the world of optimum nutrition for dogs!

History: How Commercial Dog Foods Came To Be

Half a century ago, giving dogs left-over food was the norm. If you had a Fido at home, you simply had to collect table scraps so the family's beloved pet could eat once or twice a day. Life was simple back then, and dogs were considered hardy members of the family that could live with less than ideal nutrition.

As the years progressed and values changed, people slowly realized that canines needed the right kind of nutrition, the same way that people need a balanced diet in order to live long, productive lives…and to escape the plight of modern day diseases like hypertension, diabetes and cancer.

Today, the term "dog food" equates to commercially-sold dog food. Nowadays, having a dog at home means you have to regularly stock your home with dry, semi-dry, or wet-variety dog food.

It's generally accepted that the most convenient way of feeding a Fido is to give the dog commercial dog kibble or moist dog food packets. But when did this practice begin, and why has the commercial pet food industry been sustained to such an extent that it has become a strong and dominant producer?

Well, the pet food boom actually occurred after the Second World War. With the steady increase of the country's population after the war (known as the Baby Boom) came increased consumption of meat products in the country. Increased meat consumption meant there was also a marked increase in the byproducts created by the meat processing industries.

When the raw materials for pet food became available, enterprising individuals like R. Purina developed industrial processes that paved the way to mass production of food for hogs and chickens.

From an economist's point of view, it was indeed a beautiful development in the industries. Mass-produced food pellets increased the output of hog raisers and poultry farms. The meat processing industry made the meats suitable for commercial distribution. Usable byproducts from the meat processing industry were purchased by the pet food companies.

The pet food companies adapted the various industrial processes used by food pellet manufacturers to produce commercial dog food, cat food, rabbit food, etc.

The clamor for a "balanced diet" or a steady protein source in commercial dog food meant that pet food manufacturers had no choice but to add meat to their products. Making viable, meat-based pet food wasn't a problem at all, because the technology had already been there for a while.

Slowly, the modern pet food industry developed more strategies to respond to the needs of specific markets. The strongest market is the dry pet food market.

Dry pet food or kibble is produced by combining flour (derived from various grains, including wheat), ground animal meals (meat scraps from meat processing plants are ground by heavy machines to produce a moist meal), and milk products. Some manufacturers make it a point to add vitamins and mineral content to the dry kibble, which is an important selling point used by many pet food manufacturers.

Before the actual kibble is packed and distributed to supermarkets, the carbohydrate base of the dry pet food is first spray-coated with oil (which forms the fat content of the food) and various milk products (which improves the taste of the pet food).

Dry kibble must have a carbohydrate content of at least forty percent for this existing industrial process to work -- so you now know that all dry kibble for dogs is composed of at least forty percent carbohydrates.

Let's move on to semi-moist dog food. What makes this type of dog food tick? How come it's moist, and yet it can stay "fresh" until such time that you want it to feed Fido? It all boils down to humectants.

Humectants are chemical compounds added to dog food to keep the food product wet or moist, and are also used to prevent the common chemical processes that cause spoilage.

Unlike dry kibble, semi-moist dog food makes use of at least two protein sources: ground soybeans and fresh meat (in the form of meat scraps or regular meat). Fat is also added to the final product to increase its caloric content.

Before packaging, the semi-moist dog food is molded into different shapes. Don't be deceived though: dogs couldn't care less if the food you're giving them is in shape of a heart or a chunk of meat.

Pet food manufacturers make it a point to improve the physical appearance of pet foods to attract buyers. The appearance of the food does not necessarily have a positive impact on the animal's nutrition.

Let's move on to the third type of dog food/pet food: canned food.

There are four general categories of canned dog food. The first one is called rationed dog food. Rationed dog food is the wettest variety of dog food because the base of the dog food (meat scraps, internal organs, etc.) is cooked in highly pressurized environments until a liquid state is achieved.

The resulting liquefied food is then packed in sterile cans and shipped. All-meat canned food, on the other hand, is composed mostly of animal tissue and meat byproducts. The meat base of this type of canned food is not cooked until a liquid state is achieved. Preservatives are used to maintain the physical appearance and freshness of the meat base of the canned food.

Chunky canned food and "stews" in cans are manufactured specifically to cater to the requirements of dog owners who want to give their pets moist, "fresh" food that tastes good. Unfortunately, these foods are only aesthetically pleasing to owners, and are not necessarily pleasing to the pets themselves.

Our focus should be turned to what actually goes into the creation of the dog food, and not necessarily how the food looks. In addition to preservatives and humectants, pet food manufacturers have also been known to add artificial colorants to create vibrant-looking food. The pigments used to mask the real color of the dog food are indigestible and can actually taint your dog's feces.

This is the main reason why I'm advocating that you prepare your dog's food at home so you know exactly what your beloved pet is eating. It may sound daunting at first, and it's perfectly fine if you can't implement this type of change overnight.

Alternating homemade food and dog food is a good way to balance your dog's diet. But in the final analysis, if you can invest time and energy in giving your canine companion food prepared at home, your dog has a better chance of living a longer and healthier life, especially compared to dogs that are given commercial food that only has the minimum amount of nutrients needed to sustain a healthy canine body.

Canine Nutrition Demystified

To better understand the nutritional needs of dogs, we must explore each of the major nutrients that our canine companions need in order to live long and healthy lives.

Like humans and other animals, dogs need a balanced intake of nutrients for continuous growth and tissue repair. Lack of sufficient nutrients in a dog's diet can cause stunted growth, poor healing after injury, and a decidedly shorter lifespan compared to dogs who are receiving optimum nutrition.

The Truth About Proteins

Protein is one of the most essential building blocks of mammalian life. Mammals like dogs need protein for growth, tissue repair, and regulation of biological processes.

Without protein, muscle tissue and internal organs would suffer greatly. Like humans, dogs are capable of synthesizing specific amino acids (the building blocks of protein) on their own. Other amino acids must be sourced from the dog's diet.

That's why it is not ideal to feed dogs only carbohydrate-based treats and kibbles. Too many carbohydrates and too little or no protein can do more harm than good in the long term. (This is the reason why, after the late 1800's, pet food manufacturers turned to the byproducts of meat processing plants to acquire inexpensive sources of animal protein to add to kibble, semi-moist, and canned pet food.)

A diet rich in protein is highly recommended for young pups that have already been weaned from their mother, and for young, growing dogs. Hunting dogs and other working dogs should also be given a healthy serving of protein during mealtime to keep their muscles and organs working perfectly.

However, giving a dog too much protein can create its own problems. Increased protein intake has been known to damage the dogs' kidneys, which can lead to terminal kidney failure. Too much protein has also been associated with sudden changes in a dog's temperament.

Should Fats be Avoided?

Today, fats are the most abhorred of the macro nutrients because there is a general belief that any form of fat can cause obesity and other health problems in dogs. There is a kernel of truth to this: excessive fat intake in dogs can cause obesity, especially if the dog does not regularly expend energy on a daily basis.

But this does not mean that you have to cut out fats from your pet's diet. Fat is needed for normal kidney processes. Your dog also needs fat to maintain a healthy coat and healthy skin.

With too little fat, your dog can suffer, too.

If you're feeding your dog lean dog food, one easy way to add healthy fat to your dog's diet is by adding food items with omega fatty acids. Fish is the richest source of omega fatty acids. If this isn't a feasible option for you right now, you can buy a dog supplement that has omega fatty acids. Supplementation will provide at least a minimum amount of omega fatty acids and will help your dog maintain a healthy coat.

Carbohydrates in a Dog's Diet

Since dogs are generally active, they need a clean source of carbohydrates that can be easily used for energy. There is a general consensus among veterinarians that dogs need 40 to 50 percent carbohydrates in their daily diet. Dog food companies make use of a variety of inexpensive sources of starch (carbohydrates).

If your dog is having a hard time digesting a new brand of dog food, check the ingredients. Food allergies can sometimes occur when the dog's chief source of carbohydrates is soybean in its food. (Allergies show up as excessive flatulence and other signs of indigestion.)

If your dog is allergic to soybean-based dog food (or allergic to any specific source of carbohydrates or starch), try shifting to another brand of dog food that has been manufactured with regular flour, like wheat flour. Or better yet, prepare your dog's food yourself! Recipes for homemade dog meals can be found in the second part of this book.

Indigestion in Dogs

Many commercial dog foods have a minimum of 40% carbohydrate content. Some dog foods labeled "light" are light in fat content, but have as much as 70% carbohydrate content. The evolutionary ancestors of the domestic dog do not consume high amounts of carbohydrates.

According to research, the diet of ancient hounds contains no more than thirty percent carbohydrates. The evolutionary ancestors of domestic dog breeds were able to integrate carbohydrates in their diet by consuming wild fruits such as berries, and by consuming the digestive organs of animal prey.

Dogs, being natural carnivores, have digestive systems that are highly capable of breaking down complex proteins. These complex proteins are then used for biological maintenance and energy. The same highly adaptable digestive system is capable of utilizing complex carbohydrates, as well.

So when does indigestion take place in dogs?

As we mentioned earlier, it's possible for dogs to experience indigestion because of food allergies. But food allergy is just one main cause of indigestion in pet dogs.

Indigestion can occur when there's an insufficient level of digestive enzymes in a dog's system. Different forms of sugar or carbohydrates are utilized by the dog's system through the action of specific digestive enzymes like sucrase.

When there is an enzyme deficiency, the raw material (the food) inside the dog's digestive tract is not digested properly. The food remains in the dog's system for a longer period and eventually ferments. Fermentation causes the bacterial population of the dog's digestive tract to increase exponentially. This bacterial boom also increases the water content and gas content of the dog's stomach and intestines, instantly causing symptom of indigestion.

Enzyme deficiency is caused by a variety of factors including:

The dog's age

Infection of digestive tract

Intestinal inflammation

What about dairy products, like fresh milk? Why do some dogs suffer from indigestion when they are given dairy products? Well, apart from allergy to dairy products, many adult dogs suffer from lactose intolerance because adult dogs simply do not produce the necessary enzyme to properly digest lactose, the key component of dairy products. Pups and young dogs can usually handle dairy products, but as a dog ages, the production of lactase gradually slows down and eventually ceases altogether.

In Focus: Micronutrients

Dogs need micronutrients -- vitamins and minerals -- as much as humans. Micronutrients, or trace nutrients, are needed by dogs in small amounts for tissue repair, metabolic regulation, and growth. Vitamin deficiency and mineral deficiency can easily cause malaise. This can occur if dogs are not receiving sufficient amounts of trace nutrients in their regular diet.

If you think your dog is suffering from any form of vitamin or mineral deficiency, the first and most important step is to consult with a veterinarian. Never try to self-diagnose a sick pup or adult dog, as this can prove to be disastrous. Always seek the help of qualified professionals when it comes to the health issues of your dogs.

Now, if you're in the market for some regular supplements for your dog, here are some tips:

Dogs that have bone problems or injuries benefit from calcium and phosphorous supplementation.
Note that these two minerals have to be given in balanced amounts in order to help the dog. Too much calcium or too much phosphorous can reduce the ability of the dog's body to absorb and utilize either of the minerals.

Many dog breeders and owners give pregnant dogs a daily dose of vitamin C or ascorbic acid. Do not overdo the vitamin C supplementation, because dogs can actually synthesize ascorbic acid on their own. Too much vitamin C in a dog's system will simply be excreted by the dog. Some dogs who are under stress may also be given ascorbic acid.

Is your dog suffering from dry, scaly skin due to changes in humidity and temperature? Your dog might benefit from vitamin E supplementation. Vitamin E helps in cellular regeneration, and also helps keep the dog's skin and coat in top condition.

If your dog is suffering from stress (post-operation, injury, etc.) or is having problems with flea infestation, veterinarians usually recommend B-complex supplementation. A bit of trivia about brewer's yeast (which is often given to dogs with fleas): brewer's yeast is naturally rich in B vitamins – which makes it a perfect natural remedy.

Vitamin A, vitamin D, vitamin E, and vitamin K are all fat-soluble trace nutrients that help the dog by:

Improving the dog's ability to clot blood and control bleeding

Improving and maintaining the dog's sharp eyesight

Aiding bone repair and bone growth (this is achieved through the combined action of vitamins and the mineral calcium).

Severe deficiency in the aforementioned vitamins can cause the following problems:

- Weakening of the dog's muscles
- Inability to reproduce normally
- Weakened immune system and low immunity
- Vision problems
- Inflammation of the eyes
- Rickets

Members of the B-family of vitamins are water-soluble trace nutrients and are central to the lives of healthy dogs. These vitamins allow canines to store and utilize energy properly.

Giving your dog too many vitamins can also cause problems:

Calcification can occur in vital organs such as the lungs if the dog is being given too much vitamin D supplementation.

Too much vitamin A can cause severe bone problems.

Minerals	Benefits
Calcium	Normal growth and repair of bones
Phosphorous	Normal growth and repair of bones
Potassium	Cellular maintenance, kidney health, muscle maintenance

Giving Your Dog the Right Minerals for Optimum Health

Minerals produce specific benefits when ingested by dogs. The following is a breakdown of the most vital minerals and their benefits:

Sodium	Prevents dehydration
Magnesium	Needed for the normal functioning of vital organs like the heart
Iron	Needed for production and maintenance of red blood cells
Zinc	Needed for healthy fur and normal skin
Copper	Copper is used by the dog's body to maintain a healthy coat. Copper is also needed to utilize the mineral *iron*.

Phosphorous & Calcium: How Much Is Just Right?

As we mentioned earlier, the two minerals phosphorous and calcium have to be balanced so that your dog will achieve optimum health. The following table will help you attain the proper ratio when your veterinarian tells you that mineral supplementation is necessary:

Time in the Dog's Life	Percentage of Calcium	Percentage of Phosphorous
During pregnancy	1% to 1.8%	.8% to 1.6%
Growing years	1% to 1.8%	.8% to 1.6%
"Teenage" years	.8% to 1.5%	.6% to 1.2%
Before giving birth to puppies	.8% to 1.5%	.6% to 1.2%
Regular adult	.5% to .9%	.4% to .8%

Is Your Dog Getting Enough Zinc?

If you want to maintain your dog's beautiful coat, your dog has to receive a sufficient amount of zinc. Some breeds, like huskies, develop skin problems when zinc is insufficient in their daily diet. Zinc supplementation is often given to growing pups, pregnant dams/mother dogs, and trained working dogs. The following values are from the Association of Feed Control Officials, or AAFCO.

These values show the minimum amount of zinc that a dog should receive, as well as the maximum amount before toxicity is reached. Zinc toxicity has been associated with mineral absorption issues in dogs.

Stage in the Dog's Life	Minimum Amount of Zinc	Maximum Amount of Zinc
Young puppy & growing dogs	120 mg/kg	1,000 mg/kg
Adult dogs (non-reproducing)	120 mg/kg	1,000 mg/kg
Working dogs & performance dogs	150 mg/kg	300 mg/kg

According to studies, the maximum absorption rate of zinc in dogs is only forty percent. Sometimes, zinc deficiency occurs because of genetic predispositions of some dog breeds. Increased fiber intake can also prevent the dog's system from absorbing the right amount of zinc. Excessive calcium can also prevent the proper absorption of zinc because the other mineral (calcium) actually binds with zinc.

The following food items are rich in zinc and can be mixed and matched when preparing dog food at home:

Food Item	Zinc Content
Barley	44.4 mg/kg
Corn	13 mg/kg
Oats	39.2 mg/kg
Rice	24.4 mg/kg
Wheat	20 mg/kg
Soybean meal	57.9 mg/kg

Fish meal	157 mg/kg
Meat & bone meal	101 mg/kg

Quick Tips: Canine Diet

Palatability is a big issue when it comes to canine nutrition. If Fido doesn't like the new dog food and ignores his bowl on a daily basis, you have to take steps to make the food attractive to your pet.

It's also important to observe your pet closely when you offer your dog a new dog food or new homemade meals. Is your pet digesting the food well? Does your pet feel great after his meals?

If your dog seems consistently ill after eating, your pet might be suffering from indigestion or food allergy. Excessive gas or flatulence is not normal and should be considered a warning sign that the new food is not being digested well by the animal. There is no saving the new dog food – if it's causing excessive gas, you must switch it with a tummy-friendly brand or homemade recipe.

Your dog's activity level should also be used as a measuring tool when choosing what type of food to give your dog. Some dogs like running all day long, while other dogs are accustomed to sitting around the house for most of the day.

If your dog is generally sedentary, do not give your pet dog food that is high in protein or fat. Puppies should not be given food with over twenty-five percent

protein. Slightly active adult dogs on the other hand, should only receive about twenty-two percent protein in their regular meals.

Calorie Tracking: Is Your Dog Snacking Too Much?

Giving snacks and treats to your dog is a great way to bond with your animal – but too much snacking can cause obesity and a host of other health problems. The following table will help you calculate whether a dog is consuming too many calories per day through snacking. If this is the case, cutting down on the snacks will help control your dog's weight.

Treat	Calories
Small, bite-sized dog biscuits	5 calories
Medium-sized dog biscuits	20 calories
Premium dog biscuits ("gourmet biscuits") for small dogs	70 calories
"Light" dog biscuits	15 calories
Baby carrot	3 calories

8 ounces of green beans	25 calories
.5 ounces of popcorn	54 calories
1 regular slice of cheese pizza	259 calories
1 small serving of cheese-coated French fries	399 calories
1 regular chocolate chip cookie	180 calories
1 small serving of soft ice cream	113 calories
1 large hamburger with cheese	525 calories

Due to the high caloric content of pizza, French fries, chocolate chip cookies, soft ice cream, and regular hamburgers with cheese, these food items should not be given to dogs as treats.

Canine Special: Newborn Pups At Home

Nearly everyone has experienced caring for a puppy. But what if your own dog has pups of her own? This section of the book is concerned primarily with the proper feeding and care of newborn puppies and the mother dog. Below is an average timeline that you can use to better care for new pups (and, of course, the mother dog).

1st day. Newborn pups are born. (It's a good idea to be present during the actual birthing process.) The sucking reflex of the newborn pups will allow the babies to feed from their mother.

Normally, newborn pups feed every three hours. If your pups appear firm and full of milk, your pups are doing well. Weight gain will occur in the coming weeks, although it's normal for pups to lose weight the first few days after birth. The weight loss should be no more than ten percent of the pups' original body weights.

2nd day – 3rd day. The mother dog (or "bitch") will be ready to feed. During this time, you must not give your dog regular dog kibble or canned food. What your dog needs is nutrient-rich food designed for puppies or pregnant dogs.

Choose mash or puppy food that has a high fat, protein, and carbohydrate content. Food for puppies from large breeds should not be given to dogs who have just given birth because these dog foods have generally lower nutrient content.

3rd week. The puppies will begin to pay attention to what the mother dog eats and drinks. Add a small bowl or pan of water in the box. Do not leave the pan or bowl in the box; monitor if the pups will pay any attention to it, and remove it after the pups have had their fill of water.

You can also begin feeding the pups special puppy food on the third week.

You can prepare a special mash for your three-week old pups by combining dry puppy food with a dog milk replacement formula. Prepare the formula before-hand and combine it with the dry puppy food using a blender. Blend the two ingredients until you get a fine, smooth consistency.

6th week – 7th week. Puppies are usually weaned off the milk of the mother dog after 1½ months. At this point in time, you can begin giving the pups regular dry puppy food and clean water only. The mother dog's diet should also be altered when the puppies show signs that they are no longer dependent on her milk.

Until the 6th or 7th week, the mother is still feeding on puppy food. Begin shifting the mother dog's diet once again, so that production of milk will also gradually slow down and ultimately cease altogether.

The amount of food that the mother dog receives should be slowly reduced until she is consuming the regular amount that she was accustomed to prior to pregnancy.

Minimum Nutrients in Dog Foods

In the United States, there is some regulation when it comes to commercially sold dog foods. The following minimum values were published by the Association of American Feed Control Officials.

Nutrient	Percentage/ Amount Needed by Young Dogs and Pregnant Dogs	Percentage/ Amount Needed by Adult Dogs (Non- Reproducing)
Choline	1,200 mg/kg	1,200 mg/kg
Cyanobalamin	0.022 mg/kg	0.022 mg/kg
Folic acid	0.18 mg/kg	0.18 mg/kg
Pyroxidine	1 mg/kg	1 mg/kg
Niacin	11.4 mg/kg	11.4 mg/kg
Pantothenic acid	10 mg/kg	10 mg/kg
Riboflavin	2.2 mg/kg	2.2 mg/kg
Thiamin	1 mg/kg	1 mg/kg
Vitamin E	50 mg/kg	50 mg/kg
Vitamin D	500 mg/kg	500 mg/kg
Vitamin A	5,000 IU/kg	5,000 IU/kg
Selenium	0.11 mg/kg	0.11 mg/kg
Iodine	1.5 mg/kg	1.5 mg/kg
Zinc	120 mg/kg	120 mg/kg

Manganese	5 mg/kg	5 mg/kg
Copper	7.3 mg/kg	7.3 mg/kg
Iron	80 mg/kg	80 mg/kg
Magnesium	0.04%	0.04%
Chloride	0.45%	0.09%
Sodium	0.3%	0.06%
Potassium	0.6%	0.6%
Calcium	1%	0.6%
Phosphorous	0.8%	0.5%
Linoleic acid	1%	1%
Fat content	8%	5%
Valine	.48%	.39%
Tryptophan	.2%	.16%
Threonine	.58%	.48%
Phenylalanine-tyrosine	0.89%	0.73%
Methionine-cystine	0.53%	0.43%
Lysine	0.77%	0.63%
Leucine	0.72%	0.59%
Isoleucine	0.45%	0.37%
Histidine	0.22%	0.18%
Arginine	0.62%	0.51%
Protein	22%	18%

Danger Ahead: Foods That Are Toxic to Dogs

Humans are able to safely consume a wide variety of food items, organic or otherwise. Unfortunately, the same cannot be said for dogs. Many food items that humans can consume will cause havoc in a dog's sensitive system. The biological chemistry and unique metabolic processes of the common domestic dog are the reasons why some items should never be fed to dogs:

Food Item	Reason Why It Should Not Be Given to Dogs
Beer, whiskey, rum, or any alcoholic beverage	Alcohol can cause severe intoxication in dogs, which can lead to death. It's been documented that some dogs given alcoholic beverages have gone into comas.
Avocado	All the parts of the avocado plant, including the fruit, contain the chemical compound *persin,* which has been known to cause vomiting and even loose bowel movements in dogs.

Hard bones from animals like chickens	Contrary to some popular beliefs, dogs *cannot* break down hard bones. Like humans, dogs can suffer from a punctured stomach from eating bones.
Commercial cat food	Generally, commercial cat food contains *higher* protein content than regular dog food. Some experts believe that higher concentrations of protein can cause kidney failure in dogs.
Citrus oil	Citrus oil has been known to cause vomiting in dogs.

Chocolate and caffeinated beverages	Although chocolate tastes good, it contains the compound theobromine. Dogs are *unable* to metabolize theobromine. Over time, this chemical compound can accumulate in a dog's system until a toxic level is reached. Caffeine, as well as the chemical theophylline, is present in coffee, coffee-based beverages, and teas. Both these compounds can affect the dog's heart and may also cause vomiting in some cases.

Pure fat cut from beef or pork	Too much fat can cause pancreatitis, a severe condition in both humans *and* dogs.
Large amounts of fish (in whatever form)	If the dog is not given sources of protein other than fish, the dog can suffer from vitamin deficiency (thiamine deficiency, to be exact).
Grapes and other grape-derived snacks and food items	An unknown toxin in the flesh of grapes has been known to cause kidney problems. The same goes for currants, so don't give your dogs fresh or cooked currants.

Hops (grain)	An unknown toxin in this grain causes severe allergic reactions in dogs. Documented reactions include elevated heart rate, difficulty breathing, and even death. Some dogs have been known to suffer from seizures.
Vitamin supplements for humans (with iron)	Human vitamin supplements that contain the mineral *iron* can cause havoc in the digestive tract of dogs. Organs like the liver -- and even the dog's kidneys -- can also take damage.
Macadamia nuts (fresh or otherwise)	These nuts have been known to damage the central nervous system of dogs. They may also adversely affect the digestive system.

Marijuana	Can cause vomiting and cardiovascular problems.
Spoiled food and table scraps	High levels of bacteria and molds in spoiled food can cause food poisoning and kill a dog.
Wild mushrooms	May contain potent toxins that can paralyze and kill a dog immediately after consumption.
Onions	Affect the red blood cells of dogs and also deplete the iron supply of the animal.
Persimmons	When ingested, the seeds of the persimmon can cause inflammation in the digestive tract and may also cause severe obstructions.

Raw eggs	Raw eggs contain the compound called *avidin*, which has been known to prevent the complete absorption and utility of the nutrient *biotin.* If given in large amounts, raw eggs can cause biotin deficiency, which can have a negative impact on the dog's skin and coat.
Rhubarb leaves	Oxalates found in rhubarb leaves can attack multiple organ systems, including the dog's central nervous system.
Salt	Large amount of salt can destroy a dog's delicate chemical balance.
Food items and treats with lots of table sugar	Too much sugar in a dog's diet can cause dental problems and can also lead to obesity.

Table scraps	Table scraps often contain fat and salt, and are generally empty calories with little or no nutritive value.
Yeast dough	Increases gas production in the dog's bowels, which can cause internal rupturing and death.
Xylitol	If given in excessive amounts, can cause hypoglycemia. Hypoglycemia in dogs can cause vomiting. If xylitol reaches a toxic level in the dog's system, the dog's liver may shut down completely.

Quick Reference: Growth Rate of Common Breeds

Are you having trouble figuring out how big your dog is going to get? The following quick reference will help you determine if your dog is obese, under-weight, or is growing just right.

Toy dogs – below 10 pounds (4 months), 10 pounds (most of a toy dogs' adult life).

Cocker spaniel – 10 pounds (4 months), 18-20 pounds (adult; this weight is usually maintained except for cases of obese dogs).

Bulldog – below 20 pounds (4 months), 20 pounds (8 months), 30 pounds (12 months), below 40 pounds (16 months), 40 pounds (20 months onward; this is the maintaining weight for bulldogs) .

Setters – 30 pounds (4 months), 45 pounds (8 months), 45+ pounds (12 months), 48+ pounds (adult; maintaining weight).

German shepherd – 45 pounds (4 months), 60+ pounds (8 months), 70 pounds (12 months toward adulthood; maintaining weight).

Great dane – 70 pounds (4 months), 90+ pounds (8 months), 110+ pounds (12 months), 130 pounds (16 months, adulthood; maintaining weight).

Feeding Older Dogs: The Puzzled Owner's Guide

We all love our dogs. And there is no better reward for all our hard work and concern than having a senior dog in our midst – a dog that has seen it all and has accompanied us and our families through thick and thin.

Unfortunately, senior dogs tend to be fickle eaters. This can cause obesity and malnourishment in some cases. Here are some tips to make sure that your dog stays healthy during its senior years:

1. Senior dogs are not as strong or as adaptable as younger dogs. In old age, dogs tend to lose many of their former strengths, including their ability to eat almost anything. That's why it's important to adjust the daily diet of your senior dog to fit his new needs. The food that your dog was accustomed to when it was two years old is not the same food that your dog needs in old age. We're not only talking about the type of food that your dog is being given, but also the volume and frequency of the feedings.

2. Senior dogs have weaker teeth and gums, which makes these dogs more prone to developing cavities. Avoid giving older dogs sugary treats – they might like such treats, but they're not really good for your dog's health anymore.

3. With age comes less physical activity. Like humans, dogs can suffer terribly from a sedentary lifestyle at old age. If exercise is not a feasible strategy for your dog's weight loss, then you may want to alter your dog's diet or the amount of food that your dog receives per feeding.

4. Unlike younger dogs, senior dogs need lots of fiber to keep their digestive tract healthy and clean. The daily food you serve to your dog should have around three to five percent fiber. Cut down on the fat but maintain the protein content of the food.

5. Is your older dog suffering from lack of interest in its regular food? Don't panic: an older dog ignores food for a good reason. Maybe your dog is having a hard time digesting the food? Or perhaps your dog is having trouble masticating or chewing the food? Try adjusting the portions and sizes of the food that you give your older dog and see what happens. Additional moisture in the dog food usually helps older dogs eat regularly again.

The Gradual Switch: Helping Your Dog Eat New Food

Any changes in your dog's diet should be done gradually, over a period of time. Switching his food to a new dog food brand or a homemade dog meal might cause indigestion.

Like humans, dogs have native bacteria living in their intestines. These bacteria help break down the food items that the dog eats. When your dog receives new food, the dog's intestinal flora has to adapt to the influx of new food.

A sudden change in your dog's diet might cause stomach upset because the intestinal flora will have to adjust quickly to the new diet. Any gradual shift to new dog food should take place over a period of at least five days.

If you have an older dog with digestion problems, the transition period might take as long as ten days. But after this time, you can be sure that your dog will have no problems with the new diet because you have already observed if the new diet fits your dog. If any food allergies or indigestion takes place during the transition period, you can adjust the food you are giving your dog to achieve an ideal mix.

The following graphic illustration will show you how much food you should give your dog throughout the transition period:

DAY 1 - DAY 3	DAY 1 - DAY 3	DAY 1 - DAY 3	DAY 1 - DAY 3
70% old food 30% new food	50% old food 50% new food	20% old food 80% new food	100% new food no more old food

Is Your Dog Getting Enough Water?

Generally, domestic dogs need a lot of water in order to live long, healthy lives. The common ratio is 1:2 – this simply means that if your dog eats one pound of dog food a day, your dog should drink two liters of clean water.

Your dog should have access to a clean water source so he can drink as much water as it wants. Water consumption can change if the dog is pregnant or if the dog has puppies that need to feed every few hours.

Dogs that are continually trained on a daily basis also need a lot of water throughout the day. Dehydration is a severe problem which is why you should make sure that your dog is fully hydrated the whole day.

If your dog is sick, clean water should be provided several times a day – but if the dog is vomiting, do not give the dog too much water. Consult with your veterinarian and limit water consumption until the veterinarian gives you the signal that it's okay to provide the regular amount of water again to the animal.

Part 2:
Homemade Goodness

Homemade dog food is a great alternative to commercial dog food. But before you jump in, it's very important to take the various advantages and disadvantages of giving homemade meals to your dogs into consideration. When do people usually give homemade meals to their pet dogs? Here are some of the most common reasons why people suddenly shift from commercial dog food to homemade dog food:

1. The dog has been diagnosed with a health condition that requires a special diet.

2. The dog needs more protein or calories because of continuous training.

3. The dog is allergic to most commercial dog food brands.

4. The dog is unable to fully digest commercial dog food.

5. The dog's appetite has been affected and the animal is not responding to regular feedings with commercial dog food.

6. The dog owner has decided that he/she does not want to expose the dog to the health risks associated with chemicals found in dog food, such as humectants, preservatives, artificial flavoring, etc..

As a dog owner myself, I personally prefer giving my dogs homemade meals because through these homemade meals, I can balance my dogs' protein, fat, and carbohydrate intake.

I can control portion size easily and am completely confident that what my dogs are eating is safe for consumption because I use only wholesome ingredients.

If you have the time and energy to invest in your pet's health by providing wholesome food prepared at home, then by all means, use the recipes in this book to help you decide which particular meal sets are appropriate for your dog's needs.

If these points harmonize with your own beliefs about canine nutrition, use the following guidelines to make sure that your dog's diet is indeed the best diet that you can provide:

1. Avoid giving your dog food scraps and left-overs. These food scraps provide only empty calories and may not supply enough of the vital nutrients (like vitamins and minerals) that your dog needs to maintain a healthy life.

2. If you shift from commercial dog food to homemade meals, consult with your veterinarian to make sure that you have the proper vitamin and mineral supplementation needed by your dog. Commercial dog foods have these trace nutrients integrated into the food itself. Once you shift, additional supplementation may be needed.

3. Always update yourself about the current trends in dog nutrition. Every day, researchers are finding out more and more about ideal canine nutrition. It's a good idea to keep abreast of current research so you can adjust your dog's homemade diet accordingly.

4. Be sure to observe proper cooking practices when preparing your dog's meals. Any leftover dog meals should be stored in sealed containers and re-frigerated. If you plan to keep extra meals for more than a few weeks, you can place the extra meals in sealable bags so you can freeze the containers.

5. If your dog has been eating commercial dog food for a long time, you have to slowly transition the feeding from commercial dog food to homemade meals. I have covered a sure-fire process for transitioning between foods earlier in the book. It should work for most dogs.

6. No matter how balanced and tasty a dog's diet is, your dog will not be healthy if the animal does not receive sufficient exercise. Ideally, dogs should

Treats Galore

If you want to give your dogs a healthy treat, pick from one of the following great recipes!

Creamy Banana Treat

Ingredients:

Half cup of regular peanut butter
3 bananas
2 eggs
2 tablespoons of honey
1 cup of water (you can add milk if the dog tolerates dairy products)
2 cups of flour (use wheat flour if available)
1 teaspoon of baking powder

Steps:

First, preheat your oven to 350 degrees Fahrenheit.

Combine all of the ingredients and mix well, until a smooth consistency is achieved.

On a medium-sized baking tray, place a cookie sheet and spread it evenly across the whole surface of the baking tray. Don't forget to spray the cookie sheet.

With a spoon or scoop, transfer the mixture to the cookie sheet, one spoonful/scoopful at a time.

Bake for a quarter of an hour and serve. The cookies can be placed in a sealed jar. They can also be frozen and served over the course of weeks.

Honey & Carob Delight

Ingredients:

Half cup of carob chips
1 teaspoon of vanilla flavoring
2 eggs
Quarter cup of honey
Quarter cup of canola oil
Quarter cup of water (or fresh milk)
Half cup of ground oats
Two cups of flour (wheat flour, if available)

Steps:

First, preheat the oven to 350 degrees Fahrenheit.

Combine all the ingredients in a non-reactive mixing bowl.

Spread a cookie sheet or baking sheet across your baking tray. Coat the sheet with non-stick spray.

Transfer the mixture to the cookie sheet. Place your cookies two to three inches apart.

Bake for a quarter of an hour and serve.

Brown Rice Cookies

Ingredients:

Half cup of boiled chicken (shred the chicken first)
Whole cup of brown rice (cook the brown rice before making the cookies)
2 tablespoons of regular honey
2 tablespoons of canola oil
1 egg
Half cup of baby food (anything with chicken in the label)
Half cup of chicken stock
¼ teaspoon of salt
1 teaspoon of baking powder
Quarter cup of skim milk
Two cups of flour (wheat flour if available)

Steps:

Preheat your oven to 350 degrees Fahrenheit.

Combine most of the ingredients except the rise. Stir until well blended.

Add the mixture to the rise and slowly mix, taking care to integrate a little air to the mixture.

Apply large drops of the mix to a pre-sprayed baking tray with a cookie sheet.

Bake for a quarter of an hour and serve.

Doggy Delight Cookies

Ingredients:

¼ teaspoon of salt
1 teaspoon of baking powder
Half cup of cornmeal
Two cups of flour (if available, use wheat flour)
One clove of fresh garlic
2 tablespoons of canola oil
1 egg
Half cup of chicken broth (beef broth can also be used)
Half cup of carrots (steamed or boiled carrots will do)
Half cup of chicken (or any cooked poultry; shred the meat before using)
Whole cup of mashed potatoes

Steps:

Preheat oven to 350 degrees Fahrenheit.

Combine all the ingredients and mix thoroughly in a large mixing bowl.

Spread a cookie sheet over a baking tray and spray with non-stick. Form small dollops of the mixture to make the cookies.

Bake the cookies for at least twenty minutes. Serve.

Dog Food With a Touch of Home

Ingredients:

1 tablespoon of regular honey
1 tablespoon of canola oil
1 egg
Half cup of chicken broth (beef broth can also be used)
300-400 grams of dog food (wet or moist variety)
¼ teaspoon of salt
½ teaspoon of garlic powder
Half cup of milk (use skim milk or low fat milk if available)
Two cups of flour (use wheat flour if available)

Steps:

Preheat oven to 350 degrees Fahrenheit.

Combine all the ingredients except the milk and flour in a large mixing bowl. Prepare the flour mixture next by mixing skim milk and the wheat flour (or regular flour). Add the first mix to the second mix. Combine both groups of ingredients well until a smooth and even consistency is achieved.

Place small dollops of the mix on a baking tray. Don't forget to spray the cookie sheet with non-stick spray. If the dough seems too thin or light, add more flour. You can flatten the dough with a glass or a rolling pin.

Bake the cookies for at least twenty minutes. To test for doneness, try to crack a cookie open. If the cookie is already springy, it's ready to serve.

Cheddar Dog Cookies

Ingredients:

2 tablespoons of canola oil
Whole cup of chicken stock
Whole cup of cheddar cheese, grated
¼ teaspoon of salt
¼ teaspoon of garlic powder
2 teaspoons of basil
1 tablespoon of baking powder
Two cups of flour

Steps:

Preheat your oven to 400 degrees Fahrenheit.

Combine all the ingredients except the canola oil and the chicken stock.

Spread a sprayed cookie sheet over the baking tray before applying the mix. Create half-inch cookies on the cookie sheet.

Bake the cookies for a quarter of an hour. The cookies will turn golden yellow when done.

Walnut & Cinnamon Express

Ingredients:

Half cup of walnuts, chopped
Whole apple (shred or grate the apple)
1 whole egg
2 tablespoons of canola oil
2 tablespoons of honey
1 cup of water
¼ teaspoon of salt
¼ teaspoon of cinnamon
1 teaspoon of baking soda
2 cups of flour

Steps:

Combine everything except the flour and the water. Combine the flour and water in a separate bowl. Add the first mix to the second bowl (the flour mix), and stir until a smooth consistency is achieved. Add the chopped walnuts and grated apple last.

Make half-inch dough drops on a baking tray lined with a cookie sheet. Pre-spray the cookie sheet before using.

Bake the cookies for at least twenty minutes. This recipe is suggested for dogs that need vitamin E supplementation, since tocopherol, or vitamin E, is a naturally occurring trace nutrient in walnuts. You can also add cheese to the mix if you wish.

Cookies for Healthy Eyes

Is your dog having trouble with his coat and eyesight? Try my Cookies for Healthy Eyes – the recipe is full of vitamin A -- delivered the way your dog wants it, through yummy cookies!

Ingredients:

1 carrot, grated
1 whole egg
2 tablespoons of molasses
2 tablespoons of canola oil
Half cup of water
Whole can of pumpkin
½ teaspoon of cinnamon
1 teaspoon of baking soda
2 cups of flour

Steps:

Preheat oven to 350 degrees Fahrenheit.

Combine all the ingredients except the flour and water. Create the primary flour mix in another bowl then add the first mix to the flour mix.

Prepare the baking tray by spraying a cookie sheet with non-stick spray. Add small dollops of the final mix to create the cookies.

Bake the cookies for twenty minutes and serve.

Sweet Potato Surprise

Ingredients:

Whole cup of cottage cheese
Whole cup of mashed sweet potatoes (if sweet potatoes are not available, you can use a ready-made can of pumpkin puree or pumpkin chunks instead)
1 egg
2 tablespoons of canola oil
2 tablespoons of regular honey
Half cup of milk
½ teaspoon of cinnamon (this flavoring is optional)
1 teaspoon of baking powder
2 cups of oats (instant oats)
2 cups of flour

Steps:

Preheat oven to 350 degrees Fahrenheit.

Combine all the ingredients except the flour and milk. Combine the flour and milk in a large mixing bowl and add the first mix to the flour mix.

Stir the final mixture until smooth.

Place small dollops of the final mixture onto a non-stick baking tray.

Bake the cookies for at least twenty minutes before serving or storing.

Carrot Cookies

Ingredients:

1 cup stone ground yellow cornmeal
1 tbsp vegetable oil
3/4 cup chicken broth (low or no sodium is best)
1 egg
1 tbsp grated cheddar cheese
2 tbsp minced fresh mint

Steps:

Preheat oven to 350° F.

Measure cornmeal into a small bowl.

In a sauce pan, bring the vegetable oil and chicken broth to a boil. Remove pan from the heat, stir in the cornmeal & allow to cool to the touch.

Spray the baking sheet with a non-stick cooking spray.

Once the cornmeal mixture is cool, stir in the egg, cheddar cheese and fresh mint. Shape into 1" to 1 ½ " balls. Flatten balls into cookie shapes and bake for 30 minutes.

Turn off the oven and let the cookies cool and continue to dry in the oven for one hour.

Makes 15, 2" dog cookies. Will keep for 1 week in airtight container,
3 weeks in the refrigerator and 3 months in the freezer.

Apple Crunch Pupcakes

Ingredients:

2 + 3/4 cups water
1/4 cup applesauce (unsweetened)
2 tbsp honey
1/8 tbsp vanilla extract
1 medium egg
4 cups whole wheat flour
1 cup dried apple chips (unsweetened)
1 tbsp baking powder

Steps:

Preheat oven to 350F.

Mix water, applesauce, honey, egg, and vanilla together in a bowl.

Add remaining ingredients and stir until well blended.

Pour into lightly greased muffin pans.

Bake 1 ¼ hours.

Lulu's Homemade Doggy Dream Ice Cream

Lulu loves these treats. They are like the Dogster treats you can buy in the supermarket. They are ridiculously easy to make and much cheaper!

Ingredients:

32 ounces vanilla yogurt
1 cup peanut butter

Steps:

Melt the peanut butter in a bowl in the microwave or over a pan of hot water on the stove.

Add in the yogurt and stir until blended.

Pour into cupcake papers (place them into a muffin pan to hold them still).

Note: If you have any empty Dogster cups you can use those.

Freeze.

Lulu says, "Pace around in front of the freezer until ready and then lick continuously and noisily until gone!"

YUMMY!

Lamb Pupcakes

Ingredients:

3 Cups Ground Lamb
1 Egg
1 Cup Oatmeal
1/2 Cup Ground Almonds
1 Tablespoon Cottage Cheese

Steps:

Preheat oven to 425 F.

Combine lamb, egg, oatmeal, almond meal, and cottage cheese in a bowl and mix well.

Pour into a cupcake pan with paper cups.

Bake for about 35 minutes or until browned on top and a toothpick inserted into the center of a cupcake comes out clean.

These treats must be refrigerated to keep them from spoiling.

TIP - you can substitute any meat that you want for the lamb.

Using a dehydrator

I love using a dehydrator to make healthy treats for my dogs. I originally purchased one for my own food for making dehydrated raw apple bars and dried fruit and nuts.

Then I started experimenting for the dogs. The first thing I tried was pig ears. This has been a hard adjustment for me since I have been a vegetarian for many years! But the dogs are totally crazy for these treats so I have had to get over being grossed out.

You can find many different types of dehydrators on the the market. I use the box type of dehydrator. It has 5 shelves with separate grids. You can also purchase separate teflex sheets for wet items. It also has a timer and temperature control. I keep mine in the garage partly because it makes a little humming noise which could be annoying in the house, but also because the smell drives the dogs crazy!

Note: You can find a great deal of information about dehydrators online.

Dehydrated Pig Ears

You should be able to find pig ears in a good butcher shop. I generally get mine from Penn Dutch or my local supermarket. You can always ask them to order some for you.

I generally buy 6 packs at a time which have 4 or 5 ears in each, depending on size. (I feel bad for the piggies, but try not to think about it!)

You need a good, heavy, very sharp knife. I don't wear gloves, but you could if you wished.

Place an ear on a solid cutting board and cut off all the parts that don't lay flat. Then slice the flat part into strips, each about 2 inches wide.

The smaller parts you cut off first can be cut smaller and smaller until each piece lays fairly flat.

Lay the strips onto the dehydrator sheets. You don't need the teflex sheets, just the rack. Try not to overlap the pieces.

Place the racks into the dehydrator and turn it to full heat, which will be the meat or jerky setting.

I leave mine for about 24 hours. You want the strips to be pretty hard with no soft, spongy bits left.

Store the ears in thick paper bags loosely sealed or just roll the top over. I have found that storing in airtight containers can cause mold to form.

Dehydrated Chicken Livers

This has to be one of the easiest treats in the world and one my dogs would pretty much do anything for. I only give them a couple each every other day, because too much liver can cause diarrhea.

You will need to put the teflex sheets onto the dehydrator racks for this.

I buy 6 or 7 trays of chicken livers. I open them one at a time and pour the contents into a colander or strainer laying in the bottom of the sink.

Shake the colander to get rid of the excess blood and spread the livers onto the teflex sheet. Repeat with all the sheets.

I usually find that each sheet can easily hold more than one pack of chicken livers. You will have to experiment with your own dehydrator to see how many you can do. I like to be economical and fill the dehydrator.

Set the heat to full and dehydrate for about 12 hours. Then you need to remove the livers from the teflex sheets and let them dehydrate for about 12 more hours directly on the racks. I do this by lifting the teflex sheet and turning it liver side down onto the rack. Then you can carefully roll the teflex off the liver.

As with the pig ears, these treats need to be kept in a thick paper bag or cardboard box, way out of reach of the dog. I have yet to meet a dog who doesn't totally love these!

Dehydrated Heart Slices

I usually use pig hearts but you can buy beef or veal, whichever you prefer.

Simply slice the hearts, about one quarter to a half inch thick slices work well.

Lay the slices directly onto the dehydrator rack.

Set the temperature to full, for meat or jerky.

Dehydrate for about 24 hours until hard.

Keep in paper bag or cardboard box.

Home Made Chicken Jerky Strips

Look for thin slices of chicken breast or tenders in your supermarket. Or if you don't mind slicing, any size breasts will do. Make sure they are boneless and skinless

Slice the breasts with the grain into about half inch thick slices. If you buy the thin slices they might be thin enough as they are and you can just cut them in half lengthwise.

Simply lay the strips on the racks and dehydrate on full heat for about 12 hours, depending on the thickness.

Cut one in half to check if they are done. The inside shoud be dry without any moisture and the same color all the way through.

Some people like to add seasoning before dehydrating. I never do and my dogs love these, but you can add some salt or herbs, or even fruit marinade. Whatever you think your dog would enjoy the most.

Sweet Potato Chews

Wash and dry the sweet potatoes and thinly slice. I leave the skins on, but you can peel them first if you prefer.

Lay on the dehydrator racks and dry for 3 to 12 hours until bendy. You should be able to twist them without them breaking apart.

Dry longer if your dog prefers a crispy treat.

Green Bean Snaps

Cut off the ends of the green beans and lay out on the dehydrator trays.

Dry for approximately 3 to 6 hours until they are crisp and snap apart.

Turkey Sausage Pupperoni Sticks

Buy some thin, unspiced turkey sausages and lay them out on the dehydrator trays.

Dehydrate on full for 6 to 12 hours.

They should be dry in the center when done but still a lilttle flexible.

If you like, you can make smaller bite sized treats by slicing the sausages into quarter inch rounds. They will take much less time to dry out, about 3 to 6 hours depending on thickness.

Banana Yummies

Slice firm, ripe bananas into 1/8" to 1/4" rounds.

Lay out on the dehydrator sheets and let dry for 3 to 12 hours until hard.

If you like, toss the banana bits in coconut oil or melted peanut butter before drying.

Fishy Flakes

Buy some canned bone-free tuna or whitefish.

Break into chunks and spread out onto the drying racks.

Dehydrate for 6 to 10 hours for a tasty treat.

My cats like these too!

Snacks and Quick Meals

Nutmeg Pudding

Ingredients:

¼ teaspoon of nutmeg (fresh, if possible)
¼ teaspoon of salt
2 eggs
2 tablespoons of regular honey
2 tablespoons of table sugar or molasses
Half cup of cornmeal
Two cups of milk

Steps:

Preheat your oven to 350 degrees.

Pour two cups of milk into a pot or saucepan. Switch the stove to medium heat. Let the milk simmer and eventually come to a boil.

When the milk starts boiling, reduce the stove's heat and slowly add the cornmeal. Stir regularly so that the cornmeal integrates well with the milk.

Add the sweetening agents (molasses/table sugar & honey) and the nutmeg. Lastly, add the two eggs (beat these first before using) and the ¼ teaspoon of salt.

Use a baking dish for this recipe. Bake for at least one hour before serving. The Nutmeg Pudding should be served warm (not chilled), or at least at room temperature.

Maple Appetizer

This recipe is suggested for dogs who are just recovering from illness or injury. Dogs who are just recovering usually have low or no appetites at all.

This light and very nutritious recipe will ensure that your dog gets a boosted dose of B-complex vitamins to help speed up recovery. This Maple Appetizer is also a good alternative snack for dogs that are allergic to food items with wheat, since millet is not related to wheat and does not contain compounds like gluten.

Ingredients:

½ teaspoon of cloves (ground)
Whole teaspoon of cinnamon
Half cup of maple syrup
¼ teaspoon of salt
Three cups of water
Whole cup of millet

Steps:

Preheat your oven to 350 degrees Fahrenheit.

Brush fresh butter over a medium-sized baking dish.

Cook the ingredients in a saucepan before pouring them into the baking dish. When the ingredients come to a boil, the mix is ready for the oven.

Bake the pudding mix for at least forty-five minutes before serving warm.

Tofu & Honey Heaven

Tofu is produced from soybean, one of the top sources of usable protein in the vegetable kingdom. You can give Tofu & Honey Heaven as a special treat to your dog. If your dog already has enough calories in his diet for the day, reduce the honey content of the treat by half.

Ingredients:

Half cup of regular honey
Two cups of canola oil
3 tablespoons of sesame seeds (for sprinkling)
2 tablespoons of cornstarch
Sixteen ounces of fresh tofu

Steps:

Slice the tofu into regular, thin pieces. Fry both sides of each slice of tofu until you achieve a golden brown color. The tofu slices should also be a little crunchy, but not too dry.

Drain the oil from the tofu by applying paper towels.

Place all the cooked tofu in your dog's dish or bowl. Pour the honey over the cooked tofu slices.

Sprinkle three tablespoons of cornstarch over the finished snack.

Sweet Pumpkin Snack

Ingredients:

Half cup of sliced apples
Quarter cup of honey
Half cup of water
Whole pumpkin (a medium-sized pumpkin will do)

Steps:

Preheat your oven to 350 degrees Fahrenheit.

Slice the whole pumpkin in two. Remove the seeds and any stringy material you may find inside. Wash the pumpkin thoroughly to remove any chemicals from the skin. Do not remove the skin of the pumpkin as this is a good source of dietary fiber.

Slice the pumpkin into cubes – each cube should be about 1 ½ to 2 inches long.

Combine honey and water in a medium saucepan. Cook until smooth, honeyed syrup is formed.

When the syrup is done, add the sliced apples and cook for ten minutes or less. Do not overcook, as the sugar in the honey can burn easily in high temperatures.

Place all the pumpkin slices in a baking bowl or baking dish and bake for at least one hour.

When the pumpkin is done, pour the apple and honey mix on top and serve warm.

Spicy Pie

Ingredients:

1 pie crust (at least nine inches across)
Quarter teaspoon of cloves (ground)
Quarter teaspoon of ginger (ground)
Half teaspoon of allspice (ground)
Quarter teaspoon of salt
2 whole eggs (separate the yolk from the egg white)
Three sweet potatoes (cook these first before using)

Steps:

Preheat your oven to 350 degrees Fahrenheit.

Remove the skin of the cooked sweet potatoes.

In a mixing bowl, mash the sweet potatoes until all chunks have disappeared.

Add two egg yolks to the sweet potatoes, along with the threes spices.

Place egg whites in a separate bowl and beat with a fork or hand-held beater until stiff peaks are formed.

Add one tablespoon of the beaten egg whites to the cooked sweet potato mix.

Pour the mix unto the pie crust and flatten evenly with a spoon.

Bake for at least forty minutes, slice and serve.

Beef & Cabbage Salad

Ingredients:

Quarter cup of parsley
5 cooked potatoes (use small or young potatoes)
Whole cup of beef (cooked well)
Half a cabbage (shred the cabbage first)
¼ teaspoon of salt
Quarter cup of balsamic vinegar
Egg yolk
1 teaspoon of mustard or Dijon mustard
1 teaspoon of garlic (minced finely)
1 cup of olive oil

Steps:

Create the dressing for this salad by combining egg yolk and all the other ingredients, except the cabbage and potatoes.

Arrange the pieces of cabbage and sliced potatoes on a plate. Add the beef next.

Pour the dressing over the finished salad and serve.

Doggy Tuna Salad

This recipe is recommended for overweight dogs that have been given a high-fat diet for a long time. Overweight dogs usually have a shorter lifespan than average-weight or optimum-weight dogs, which is why it's a good idea to start trimming excess weight now, while your dog is still strong.

Ingredients:

7 ounces of canned tuna
1 teaspoon of sugar
1 tablespoon of mustard or Dijon mustard
Quarter cup of red wine vinegar
Half cup of olive oil
Quarter cup of white onion optional; if your dog does not like onions, do not add chopped onions to the Doggy Tuna Salad)
1 medium-sized carrot (slice the carrot first)
Whole head of cabbage

Steps:

Remove the water from the tuna and pour the flakes in a separate container.

Combine the onions, sugar, and other ingredients with the tuna flakes.

Arrange the cabbage leaves in a bowl.

Top the cabbage leaves with the first mixture and serve to your dog.

Baked Veggie Roll

Ingredients:

Half cup of cheddar cheese, grated
Whole cup of stock (chicken or beef)
Half cup of yogurt (low fat variety)
Pinch of ground pepper (black or white)
¼ teaspoon of salt
½ teaspoon of oregano
1 teaspoon of parsley (use fresh parsley if available)
Whole cup of rice (cook the rice before using)
Whole cup of chicken (cooked; shredded)
Separated cabbage leaves (7 to 10 leaves will do)

Steps:

Preheat your oven to 350 degrees Fahrenheit. Use the largest baking dish you have.

Remove the hard portion of the separated cabbage leaves. Fill a pot with water and bring the water to a boil. When the water is already boiling, add the cabbage leaves.

Allow the cabbage leaves to soften enough so you can easily roll the leaves without breaking apart the leaf's structure.

Line a bowl or large plate with paper towels and transfer each of the simmered leaves unto the paper towel lining. Allow the paper towels to absorb the moisture.

Combine all the other ingredients in a mixing bowl. Mix well.

To bind the ingredients together, use the low fat yogurt. Add just enough of this ingredient to produce a thick mix. (Too much yogurt will cause the mix to fall apart when molded with the cabbage leaves.)

For each cabbage leaf, add two to three tablespoonsful of the primary roll mix.

Roll each filled cabbage leaf, taking care to 'lock' the cabbage leaf by tucking in the corners.

Place the rolled cabbage leaves in a baking dish, side by side.

Pour the stock of your choice in the baking dish. The water level must reach at least one inch before you can cook the veggie rolls.

As a finishing touch, add the cheese on top.

Cover the baking dish and allow the veggie rolls to cook for at least thirty minutes.

Serve the veggie rolls warm to your dog.

Soup of Champions

Ingredients:

Whole egg
2 tablespoons of cornstarch (Dissolve the cornstarch in ¼ cup of water first.)
2 tablespoons of tamari sauce
2 tablespoons of parsley
Two scallions (chop these first)
16 ounces of regular tofu
Six to seven cups of regular chicken stock

Steps:

Combine all the ingredients in a pot or medium saucepan.

Turn the heat up to medium-heat and allow the mix to simmer for a few minutes.

After a quarter of an hour, add the egg and allow the egg to cook thoroughly.

Serve warm.

Suave Coat Booster

This recipe produces a puree that can be added to any other dog food you're giving your dog. This puree will help heal any skin problems and will also help keep your dog's coat shiny and healthy.

Ingredients:

2 tablespoons of corn oil
Half clove of garlic (crush the garlic before using)
1 tablespoon of brewer's yeast
1/3 cup of wheat germ
1 egg (boil the egg for 4 minutes, keep the shell)
Whole cup of chicken stock

Steps:

Combine all the ingredients in a blender.

Blend the ingredients for a minute and store.

Pour a small amount of the puree on top of your dog's regular meals.

Festive Dog Food

Ingredients:

4-5 slices of bread (cut into small, 1-inch pieces)
2 tablespoons of tamari sauce
Six whole cups of chicken or beef stock
¼ teaspoon of salt
1 tablespoon of oregano
1 whole stalk of fresh celery
2 whole carrots (chop these first before using)
2 onions (chop these first before using)
4 potatoes (sliced into slim, 1-inch thick pieces)
2 tablespoons of butter (non-salted or low salt)
Half kilo of gizzard

Steps:

Fill a pot with water and bring the water to a boil. Pour the gizzards in the water and let the organ meats cook for at least 45 minutes.

When the gizzards are cooked, strain the meat but don't throw away the resulting stock. Slice the cooked gizzards.

Combine the chicken stock and the soup from the gizzard. Add the sliced gizzards and let the soup cook for an additional ten minutes.

Get a medium sized saucepan and put some butter on the pan. Switch the stove to medium heat and cook the butter. Add the vegetables and let the vegetables cook for a few minutes.

When the vegetables are cooked, add the vegetables to the soup. The resulting nutritious soup is now ready to be served warm to your dog.

Egg Noodle Deluxe

Ingredients:

2 eggs (boil the eggs for four to five minutes then remove the shells before chopping)
Whole cup of bread crumbs
2 tablespoons of parsley
Half cup of cheddar cheese (grate the cheese first)
Whole cup of chicken stock
Two cups of milk
Half kilo of egg noodles
Half kilo of chicken or turkey (lean cuts only)
4 tablespoons of butter (low salt or non-salted only)

Steps:

Preheat your oven to 350 degrees Fahrenheit.

Add butter to a medium saucepan and cook the shredded turkey or chicken for a few minutes.

Cook the egg noodles by following the manufacturer's instruction on the back of the pack.

In another pan, combine the milk and the chicken stock. When the mixture is simmering, add the cheddar cheese. Cook the mix until the grated cheddar cheese has melted completely.

In a third pan, cook the bread crumbs by toasting the crumbs with butter. Cook for a few minutes and set aside.

Mix the resulting cheese soup with the cooked chicken or turkey.

Pour the chicken-cheese mix into a baking dish. Add the sliced eggs and the buttery, toasted bread crumbs.

Bake the dish for at least 45 minutes. Serve warm.

Lemony Halibut

Ingredients:

Cooked rice
2 tablespoons of cilantro
Whole cup of tomato puree (commercial or homemade)
Lemon juice (equivalent to a whole lemon's worth)
Quarter cup of olive oil
1 kilo of halibut steak (deboned)
Steps:

Broil the halibut steaks and season with fresh lemon juice. Use the olive oil, too. Apply with a regular barbecue basting brush.

Cook each side for approximately twelve minutes, or until the flesh of the halibut flakes easily with a fork.

Pour the tomato puree into a medium-sized saucepan and simmer for a few minutes.

Place the cooked halibut steaks in your dog's bowl and pour the puree over the halibut. Add cooked rice as well.

Seafood Appetizer

Ingredients:

Cooked rice
1 tablespoon of tamari sauce
2 tablespoons of margarine
2 scallions (chop these first)
Whole quart of fish stock
1 kilo of squid

Steps:

Wash and the clean the squid.

Add a quart of fish stock to a pot and bring the fish stock to a boil. Add the cleaned squid and cook for 30 minutes.

When the squid is cooked, add the rest of the ingredients.

Serve warm with cooked rice.

Liver for Life

Ingredients:

Dry dog kibble
Bay leaf
Pepper
Whole cup of chicken stock
1 onion (chopped)
3 tablespoons of bacon dripping
1 kilo of beef liver (slice the liver into small pieces first)
Half cup of flour

Steps:

Add a little pepper to the flour to add flavor.

Coat the sliced beef liver pieces with the peppery flour.

Place bacon drippings in a Dutch oven and allow the fat to melt.

Add the coated beef liver slices to the melted bacon drippings.

Add the rest of the ingredients and let everything cook for at least one hour.

Pour the liver and the resulting sauce over your dog's regular food.

Beef & Veggie Pie

Ingredients:

Whole cup of chicken stock
2 tablespoons of cornstarch
1 commercial pie crust (nine inches)
1 egg (hard-boiled; remove the shell and slice)
Half cup of beef (ground, low fat)
Two cups of cooked brown rice
1 teaspoon of parsley
1 teaspoon of thyme
1 teaspoon of oregano
Whole cup of broccoli
1 tablespoon of canola oil

Steps:

Preheat your oven to 400 degrees Fahrenheit.

Cook the vegetables for a few minutes in a pan or skillet. Add the oil before adding the vegetables.

Combine the vegetables with the spices (thyme, oregano, parsley).

Dissolve the cornstarch before adding to the chicken stock.

Transfer the cooked vegetables to the pie crust. Pour the chicken stock, too.

Bake the pie for at least 30 minutes. Serve warm.

Chili Doggy Style

Ingredients:

4 chicken breasts
1 cup of kidney beans, drained
1 cup of black beans, drained
1 cup of carrots, diced
1/2 cup of tomato paste
4 cups of chicken broth

Steps:

Chop the chicken breasts into small pieces and fry over a mdeium heat until just cooked.

Put all the ingredients, including the cooked chicken, into a large pot and warm through over a medium heat for about 10 minutes.

Cool before serving.

Can be kept in the refrigerator for up to 5 days.

Rice Free Beef & Veggie Stew

Ingredients:

1 pound of beef stew meat
1 small sweet potato
1/2 cup of carrots, diced
1/2 cup of green beans, diced
1/2 cup of flour
1/2 cup of water or organic vegetable oil, plus 1 tablespoon of vegetable oil for frying

Steps:

Cook the sweet potato until tender. Dice.

Cut the beef into smal chunks and fry over a medium heat in 1 tablespoon of oil until cooked.

Remove the beef leaving all the juices in the pan. Add the flour and water slowly and stir continuously as it thickens.

Add in the cooked beef, sweet potatoe, carrots and green beans. Stir together and cook for about 10 minutes until the carrots are tender.

Cool before serving.

Remainder can be kept for up to 5 days in the refrigerator.

References

Books

Anson, Suzan Bone Apetit! Gourmet Cooking For Your Dog (New York: New Chapter Press, Inc.) 1989

Fortunato, Lisa Everything Cooking for Dogs (Massachusetts: F + W Publications) 2007

Liou, Wendy Divine Dog Treats (USA: iUniverse Press) 2010

Shenk, Patrica Home Prepared Dog & Cat Diets, Second edition (Iowa: Wiley-Blackwell) 2010

Van Rosendal, Julie In the Dog Kitchen: Great Snack Recipes for Your Dog (Canada: Touchwood Editions) 2005

Web

Carbohydrates as Energy Sources in Dog Foods
http://www.peteducation.com/article.cfm?c=2+1659+1661&aid=655 [Accessed 23 February 2011]

Choosing a Dog Food
http://www.peteducation.com/article.cfm?c=2+1659+1661&aid=2661 [Accessed 23 February 2011]

Dog Food Labels
http://www.peteducation.com/article.cfm?c=2+1659+1661&aid=668 [Accessed 23 February 2011]

Dog Food Standards by the AAFCO
http://www.peteducation.com/article.cfm?c=2+1659+1661&aid=662 [Accessed 23 February 2011]

Dry, Semi-moist, or Canned Pet Food: What is Best?
http://www.peteducation.com/article.cfm?c=2+1659+1661&aid=3328 [Accessed 23 February 2011]

Fats: Nutritional Requirements & Obesity
http://www.peteducation.com/article.cfm?c=2+1659+1661&aid=664 [Accessed 23 February 2011]

Fiber in Dog Foods
http://www.peteducation.com/article.cfm?c=2+1659+1661&aid=656 [Accessed 23 February 2011]

Foods to Avoid Feeding Your Dog
http://www.peteducation.com/article.cfm?c=2+1659+1661&aid=1030 [Accessed 23 February 2011]

Government Regulation of the Pet Food Industry
http://www.peteducation.com/article.cfm?c=2+1659+1661&aid=2645 [Accessed 23 February 2011]

How Pet Foods are Manufactured
http://www.peteducation.com/article.cfm?c=2+1659+1661&aid=2653 [Accessed 23 February 2011]

Mineral Supplementation in Dog Foods
http://www.peteducation.com/article.cfm?c=2+1659+1661&aid=2594 [Accessed 23 February 2011]

Protein Requirements for Good Nutrition
http://www.peteducation.com/article.cfm?c=2+1659+1661&aid=702 [Accessed 23 February 2011]

Switching Your Pet to a New Food
http://www.peteducation.com/article.cfm?c=2+1659+1661&aid=1155 [Accessed 23 February 2011]

Treats are Better Than Table Scraps
http://www.peteducation.com/article.cfm?c=2+1659+1661&aid=834 [Accessed 23 February 2011]

Water: A Nutritional Requirement
http://www.peteducation.com/article.cfm?c=2+1659+1661&aid=716 [Accessed 23 February 2011]

How big is my dog going to get?
http://www.peteducation.com/article.cfm?c=2+1659+1651&aid=1068 [Accessed 23 February 2011]

Caring for Newborn Puppies & Their Mother
http://www.peteducation.com/article.cfm?c=2+1659+1651&aid=916 [Accessed 23 February 2011]

Puppy Food Standards by the AAFCO
http://www.peteducation.com/article.cfm?c=2+1659+1651&aid=703 [Accessed 23 February 2011]

Food Allergies:Common Foods
http://www.peteducation.com/article.cfm?c=2+1659+1664&aid=1028 [Accessed 23 February 2011]

Food Allergies and Food Intolerance
http://www.peteducation.com/article.cfm?c=2+1659+1664&aid=143 [Accessed 23 February 2011]

Are high protein diets harmful to a dog's kidneys?
http://www.peteducation.com/article.cfm?c=2+1659+1664&aid=1104 [Accessed 23 February 2011]

Homemade Diets
http://www.peteducation.com/article.cfm?c=2+1659+1664&aid=672 [Accessed 23 February 2011]

Nutritional Needs of Senior Dogs
http://www.peteducation.com/article.cfm?c=2+1659+1664&aid=698 [Accessed 23 February 2011]

Calcium & Phosphorous Requirements for Dogs
http://www.peteducation.com/article.cfm?c=2+1659+1662&aid=652 [Accessed 23 February 2011]

Glucosamine & Chondroitin for Hip Dysplasia & Arthritis in Dogs
http://www.peteducation.com/article.cfm?c=2+1659+1662&aid=670 [Accessed 23 February 2011]

Mineral Supplementation in Dog Foods
http://www.peteducation.com/article.cfm?c=2+1659+1662&aid=2594 [Accessed 23 February 2011]

Essential Minerals
http://www.peteducation.com/article.cfm?c=2+1659+1662&aid=684 [Accessed 23 February 2011]

Omega Fatty Acids: Sources, Effects, and Therapeutic Uses in Dogs
http://www.peteducation.com/article.cfm?c=2+1659+1662&aid=666 [Accessed 23 February 2011]

Potassium Requirements in Dogs
http://www.peteducation.com/article.cfm?c=2+1659+1662&aid=700 [Accessed 23 February 2011]

Sodium & Chloride Requirements
http://www.peteducation.com/article.cfm?c=2+1659+1662&aid=686 [Accessed 23 February 2011]

Fat Soluble Vitamins: A, D, E & K in Dogs
http://www.peteducation.com/article.cfm?c=2+1659+1662&aid=710 [Accessed 23 February 2011]

Water Soluble Vitamins - Vitamin C & Vitamin B Complex in Dogs
http://www.peteducation.com/article.cfm?c=2+1659+1662&aid=712 [Accessed 23 February 2011]

Vitamin Supplements
http://www.peteducation.com/article.cfm?c=2+1659+1662&aid=714 [Accessed 23 February 2011]

Zinc Requirements in Dogs
http://www.peteducation.com/article.cfm?c=2+1659+1662&aid=718 [Accessed 23 February 2011]

Calorie Content of Foods People Use as Dog Treats
http://www.peteducation.com/article.cfm?c=2+1659+1660&aid=654 [Accessed 23 February 2011]

www.ingramcontent.com/pod-product-compliance
Lightning Source LLC
Chambersburg PA
CBHW081258040426
42452CB00014B/2549